Make Your Own
Cute and Easy Pompoms

When you wrap these three colored yarns together...

Creative Publishing
international

Contents

You can make flower-patterned pompoms like this one.

Most of the pompoms made in the past were single-colored or used multi-colored yarn. However, this book will introduce you to the wonders of flower, stripe, and butterfly-patterned pompoms. Moreover, within these pages you will see that just by slightly morphing the shape of a pompom, you can create an apple or a hedgehog. Let's flip through the pages now. We think that you will surely want to make your own pompoms – cute patterned pompoms are waiting for you.

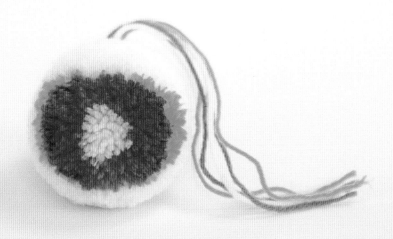

See – p. 65

Multicolored - 1 See – p. 82~83

See – p. 83~85 **Multicolored - 1** 05

See – p. 61~64, p. 74 **Butterflies (Semicircular Pompom)** 07

08 **Flowers – Small Pink Flower**   See – p. 65

See – p. 65 **Flowers – Red and Pink**

See – p. 65~67 **Flowers**   11

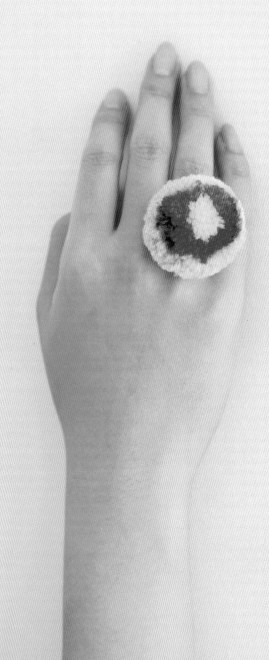

Flowers – Vermillion Petal See – p. 67

See – p. 67 **Intricate Flowers - Carnation** 13

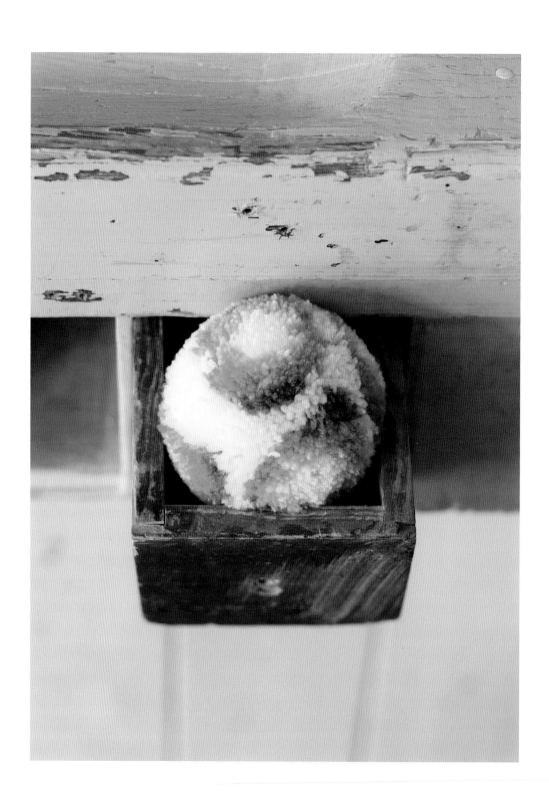

14 **Flower Bouquets – Blue** See – p. 68

$$\frac{4}{3}\pi r^3$$

See – p. 68 **Intricate Flowers - Dahlia**

17

See – p.86~87 **Droplets** 19

Simple Stripes See – p.75

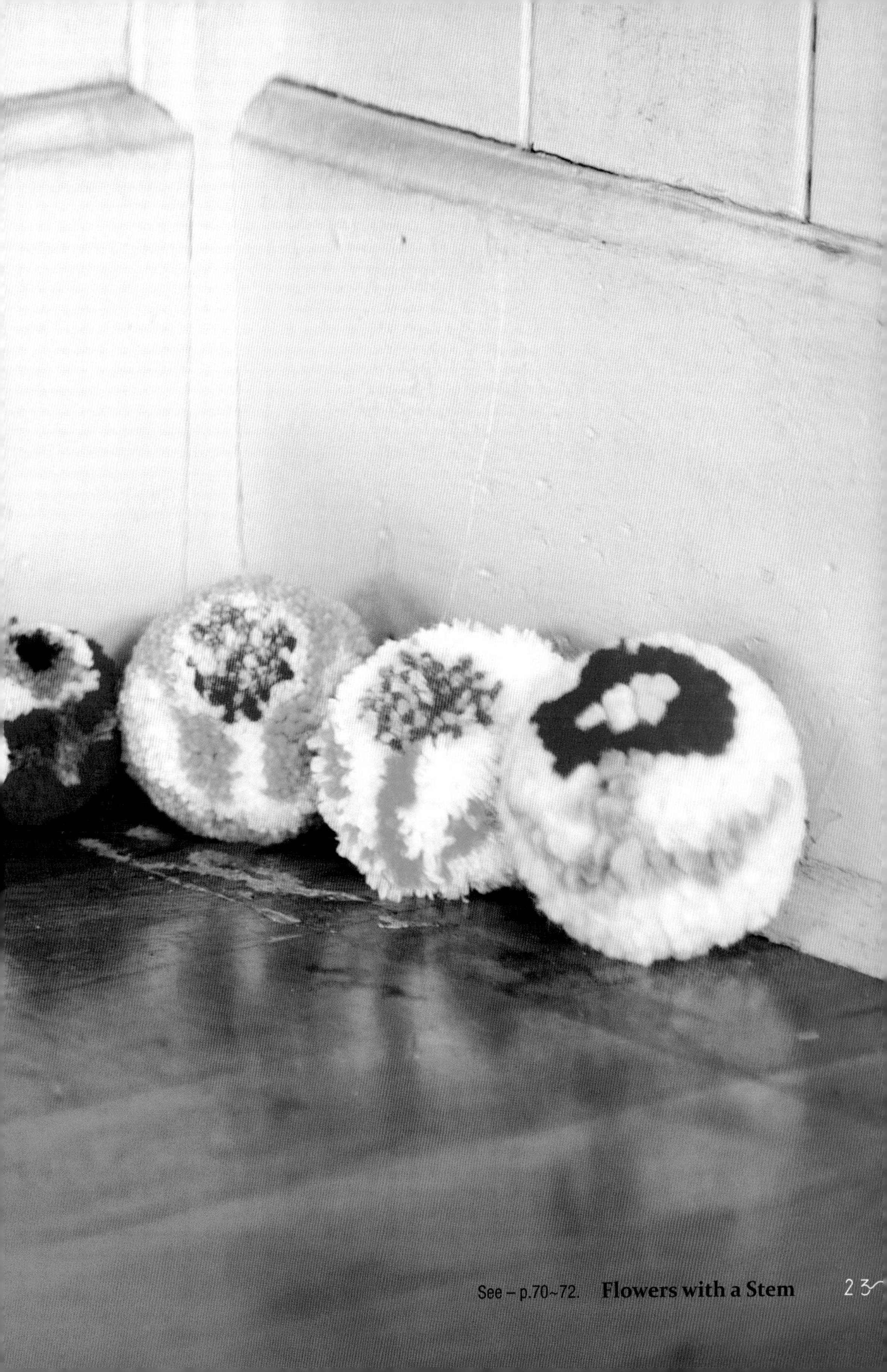

See – p.70~72. **Flowers with a Stem**

24 **Joined Yellow Pompoms with Pink Flowers** See – p.59~60, p.69

See – p.70 **Joined Blue Pompoms with Pink Flowers** 25

Semi-circular Pompoms   See – p.72

See – p.72~73 **Semi-circular Pompoms – Pompom Brooch** 27

See – p.73 **Corsages**

りんご　つくり方P.90

See – p.90 **Apples** 35

Wreaths See – p.78

See – p.79 **Snowman**

37

Christmas Tree Ornaments   See – p.80

Earrings See – p.81

See – p.82 **Necklaces** 41

Scarfs   See – p.76

See – p.76~77 **Bear Scarf, Bunny Bracelet**

43

46   **Hamburger**   See – p.89

See – p.89 **Letters**

47

Dharma Dolls   See – p.91

Hedgehogs and Ladybugs   See – p.93~94

See – p.94 **Summer Scarfs** 51

Using Different Materials See – p.94~95

See – p.95 **Pompom-sets**

Pompom Making Tools

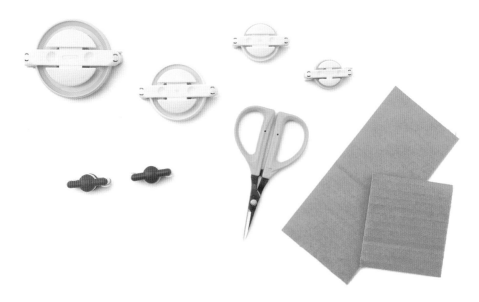

You do not need any special tools for making pompoms. All you need are your favorite strands of yarn, a cardboard template (about 5mm thickness), and a pair of scissors. A pompom maker (four shown in the photo above, two below) might also come in handy. Of course, a pair of scissors is also very important. However, if they are dull it will be difficult to cut the yarn so we do recommend that you use sharp scissors like sewing shears or craft scissors. Any cardboard scraps you have laying around will work for your cardboard templates. We recommend pieces of cardboard that are about 5mm/0.20in in thickness for easy handling. Whether you prefer to use a pompom maker or a cardboard template, once you have one of them in hand you are all set to go.

How to Make a Cardboard Template

When you make pompoms using a cardboard template, prepare the template in advance. The width of the necessary template is listed with its wrapping pattern on pages 65-95. Cut a piece of cardboard, as seen in the photo on the right. There is no specific length for cardboard templates.

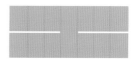

For round pompoms:
Cut long slits in the template on each side, leaving 7mm/0.28in to 8mm/0.3in at the center.

For semicircular pompoms:
Cut slits that are about 5 mm long on each end.

About Yarn

Since the number of wraps you use depends on thickness of yarn, the type of yarn used for each wrapping pattern is given. Fine yarn is used for the majority of works in this book. For all yarns, the type of yarns and thickness are shown at the bottom of each wrapping pattern page. Please prepare your yarns accordingly. Also, if the thickness of the yarn that you are going to use is twice the size written on the wrapping pattern, decrease the number of wraps by half.

Type of Yarn

SUPER FINE
1
SUPER FIN
Super Fino

FINE
2
FIN
Fino

LIGHT
3
LEGER
Ligero

MEDIUM
4
MOYEN
Medio

BULKY
5
BULKY
Abultado

SUPER BULKY
6
SUPER BULKY
Super Abultado

01 How to Make Pompoms Using Cardboard Templates

The most basic method is explained here. Here, we will make the flower pompom pictured on the far right of page 11. The wrapping pattern (right) is drawn in the shape of a pompom maker. For a cardboard template, please refer only to the top half of the wrapping pattern.

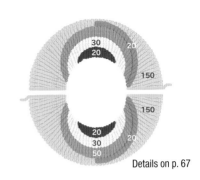

Details on p. 67

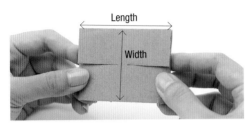

○1 The width specified in the wrapping pattern is 6cm/2.4in, so prepare 6cm/2.4in x approx. 9cm/3.5in (length does not matter particularly) piece of cardboard and put slits in both ends. (Refer to p.54)

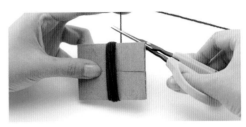

○2 Just referring to the top half of the wrapping pattern, start wrapping the yarn that is specified at the center of the pattern. Wrap 20 rounds of brown yarn around the center of the cardboard template and cut the yarn. (See p.63 for the yarn fastening method)

○3 As per the wrapping pattern, wrap 30 rounds of white yarn on top of the wrapped brown yarn. Next wrap 50 rounds of pink yarn. As you can see in the wrapping pattern, wrap white and then pink yarn to cover the yarn underneath completely.

○4 Covering about half of the pink yarn wrap 20 rounds of green yarn then cut the yarn.

○5 Lastly, wrap 150 rounds of beige yarn so that all the yarn underneath is covered.

○6 When the yarn is fully wrapped according to the pattern, cut 60cm/23.6in of beige yarn and fold it in half. Put the 60cm/23.6in strand through the slits of the cardboard template.

○7 Tie a tight knot in the strand of beige yarn at the center of the template. Tie the knot until it wedges into the wrapped yarn as much as it can. Careful, if the tie is loose the pompom itself will become loose and can easily fall apart.

○8 Snip across both edges of the template. Using scissors vertically start to make incisions near the middle little by little. This makes it easier to snip, as opposed to snipping from the edge.

○9 After snipping the yarn, the flower pattern will pop right out. It is okay if the shape of flower is slightly off. It can be fixed in the later steps.

1○ After snipping both sides, twist and pull the cardboard template to break it and then remove it from the pompom. It is easily removed when the center of cardboard template is completely torn.

11 This is what the untrimmed pompom looks like. Even without trimming, it still looks cute. (For the scarf on p.42, and the flower pompom on p.16, use untrimmed pompoms)

12 Trim the pompom down. You can trim it vigorously. Trim the pompom to make it round by consistently gauging the shape as a whole.

13 If the pattern is speckled, move the yarn around using the tip of your scissors to adjust. You should be able to move the yarn around easily and make the pattern more beautiful.

14 After adjusting the pattern, trim any yarn that is still sticking out. When the pompom reaches its desired shape, it is complete. The pompom can be tied to an object using the trailing piece of yarn or you can make an accessory by attaching metal fittings.

02 How to Make Pompoms Using Pompom Makers

This section will explain the method for making basic round pompoms using the Clover Pompom Maker. Similar to the previous section, let's make the far right flower pompom on page 11.

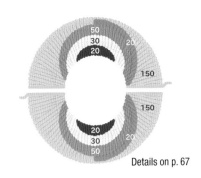

Details on p. 67

○1 Using the yellow color Clover Pompom Maker – Small (45 mm/1⅝ inches), start wrapping the yarn specified at the center in the pattern. Open the maker, wrap 20 rounds of brown around the center, and then cut the yarn. (See p.54 for yarn fastening method)

○2 According to the pattern, wrap 30 rounds of white yarn over the brown. As you can see in the pattern, wrap the yarn so that it covers the yarn underneath completely.

○3 Next, wrap 50 rounds of pink yarn.

○4 In order to cover about half of the pink yarn, wrap 20 rounds of green yarn. Then, cut the green yarn.

○5 Lastly, wrap 150 rounds of beige yarn so that it covers all of the yarn underneath and then close the arm. If you use enough yarn to make it hard to close the arm, because of the sheer volume of yarn, the pompom should be nice and plump.

○6 Wrap yarn onto the other arm according to lower half of the wrapping pattern. (This pompom has the same pattern on the front and back so the wraps are the same on each arm. If the pattern is different on the front and back wrapping will be different.)

○7 While the arms are still closed, cut the outer edge of the yarn.

○8 After cutting, the pattern will begin to appear. It is okay if the shape of the flower is a little disorderly. It can be fixed in later steps.

○9 Cut a 60cm/23.6in piece of beige yarn and fold it in half. Tie the pompom very tightly around the center with the beige yarn.

1○ After securing the pompom, open both arms and separate the pompom maker from the pompom you just made.

11 This is an untrimmed pompom. Even without trimming, it still looks cute. (For the scarf on p.42, and the flower pompom on p.16, use untrimmed pompoms.)

12 Trim the pompom. Beforehand, crumple the pompom gently. This makes all the yarn straighten out for easier trimming.

13 Similar to the instructions on p.56, vigorously trim the pompom and adjust the design using the tip of your scissors.

14 After adjusting the design, trim excess yarn. When the pompom reaches the desired shape, you are done. The pompom can be tied to an object using the trailing piece of yarn or you can make it into an accessory by attaching your favorite metal fittings.

03 How to Join Pompoms Together

Joining pompoms together makes them look very different. When you use a pompom maker, before removing the maker to trim the pompoms, join them by drawing a long strand of yarn around the center of each pompon. This method will be explained on this page.

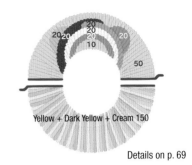

Yellow + Dark Yellow + Cream 150

Details on p. 69

○1 According to the wrapping pattern, make one of the pompoms. When you tie the pompom at the center, leave the trailing end of yarn at the "back" of the pompom.

○2 Prepare a strand of yarn about 1m in length and fold it in half. Without removing the pompom maker from your pompom, use the 1m long strand of yarn to tie the center again.

○3 This time, when you tie the yarn leave the trailing end of yarn out the "side" as shown.

○4 Remove the pompom maker. As shown in the photo above, one strand of yarn is exiting from the side and the other is trailing from the rear of the pompom.

○5 Make another pompom using the same wrapping pattern. Similar to above, leave the trailing end of yarn at the rear when you tie the pompom. Then tie the long strand of yarn trailing from the first pompom around the center of the second pompom.

○6 Lay the first pompom's long strand of yarn along the center of second pompom. At this point, adjust the pompoms' positions to make sure the flower designs face the same direction.

O7 Tie the long strand of yarn around the side of second pompom. Do not tie it tight or double. Leave it somewhat loose so that it can be tightened later.

O8 Remove the pompom maker. If it is hard to open the arm because the pompoms are touching each other you may need to force it a bit.

O9 The photo above shows you how it should look when the pompom maker is removed.

1 O Pull the long strand of yarn, which you tied loosely in the step above, forcefully and tie it tightly so that the two pompoms are securely touching each other.

1 1 Make a third pompom in the same manner as the second one. Tie the second and third pompoms together using the long strand of yarn trailing from the second pompom.

1 2 After removing the pompom maker from the third pompom, pull the long strand of yarn forcefully and tie it again to secure all three pompoms tightly together.

1 3 Trim all three pompoms at the same time. Trim it to make one long and narrow pompom.

1 4 Straighten the design using scissors and trim nicely to finish. Cut the long strands of yarn exiting from the side of each pompom and use the shorter trailing strand from the rear of the first pompom to make an accessory.

04 How to Make Semicircular Pompoms Using Cardboard Templates

For making brooches, the semicircular pompom comes in handy. The fan shaped wrapping pattern (right) is for using a pompom maker. However, the same pattern applies for a cardboard template as well.

Details on p. 76

○1 As per the width specified in the wrapping pattern, prepare a 3cm/1.2in x approx. 9cm/3.5in (length does not matter) piece of cardboard and cut slits about 5mm/0.2in long at both ends. (Refer to p.54)

○2 Prepare a strand of yarn about 60cm/23.6in in length and fold it in half. As shown, hook the double-up strand around both slits. If you leave the short loop of yarn on your dominant hand side, it makes later steps easier. (The photo shows a right handed person)

○3 According to the wrapping pattern, and following the photo above, wrap blue yarn onto the template. As you can see, to make the wings of butterfly you need to wrap yarn diagonally upward. To do so, make the left blue yarn base thick and then wrap the yellow wing part over this (see next step).

○4 Wrap the left blue yarn base thickly and then wrap green yarn on top of it to make antennae. At the center, wrap yellow yarn to make wings.

○5 After having completely wrapped the yarn, pull the short loop of yarn hooked on the cardboard template and make it even in length with the opposite side.

○6 Tie the two even strands of yarn tightly around the center.

○7 Using scissors cut the yarn exactly opposite from where you tied it.

○8 After cutting across the yarn, remove the cardboard template. The pompom looks disheveled at first but the design will come out clearly with trimming.

○9 Prepare a piece of felt similar in color to your butterfly. Cut it in a circle about 35mm/13.8in in diameter.

1○ Fold the felt in half and make two slits.

11 Draw the trailing ends of yarn used to tie the pompom through the slits of felt and tie firmly. Doing so secures the pompom's semicircular shape.

12 Begin trimming the pompom. About halfway through, adjust the butterfly design.

13 The photo above shows a pompom after adjusting the design. Trim further to make the pompom round.

14 It is complete when the pompom looks nice and round. You can attach your favorite metal fitting to the trailing yarn. Or prepare felt of similar size and shape to what you used for the backing and sew it directly to said backing. Then just attach a safety pin to the felt and it becomes a brooch.

05 How to Make Semicircular Pompoms Using Pom-Pom Makers

A semicircular pompom is very handy and the number of rounds you need to use is half that of round pompoms. Use the wrapping pattern (right) and only one arm of a pompom maker.

Details on p. 76

○1 Wrapping is the same as on p.55. Wrap the yarn according to the pattern. To prevent the pompom from becoming loose when changing yarns make a loop over your finger with the last round.

○2 Cut the yarn and draw the trailing end through the loop made by your finger.

○3 By pulling the end tight, the yarn will be secured. Cut the trailing end of yarn close to where it was secured. This prevents it from becoming loose and you can move on to the next step.

○4 For the light blue yarn make the left side thicker. On the right, wrap 6 rounds of green yarn to make the antennae.

○5 If you take a look at the wrapping pattern, it tells you to wrap the yarn diagonally upward to the left to make wings. In this case, make the left side of the light blue yarn thicker and then wrap yellow yarn on top to make the wings.

○6 Wrap 65 rounds of yellow yarn around the center to make wings. To do so, wrap it in between the green and light blue yarns, overlapping the light blue yarn a little.

○7 Wrap 200 rounds of light blue yarn over everything and then close the arm.

○8 Cut the outer edge.

○9 Prepare a strand of yarn about 60cm long and fold it in half. Thread the strand of yarn through the center and tie it securely.

1○ Remove the pompom maker.

1 1 As instructed on p.62, attach a piece of felt on the rear side.

1 2 Before trimming the pompom looks so disheveled that it might make you uneasy. Don't worry! After trimming it will become nice and round.

1 3 Trim the pompom and adjust the design using the tip of your scissors.

1 4 Trim nicely to finish. When you remove the pompom maker, the look of pompom may be undesirable. However, just by trimming and adjusting the design it will become pretty like this.

Wrapping Patterns

Flowers – Pink Peony
(See p.3)
Type of Yarns: Fine – Pink, White, Green
Cardboard Template Width: 6cm/2.4in
Clover Pompom Maker: Small (Yellow, 1-5/8")

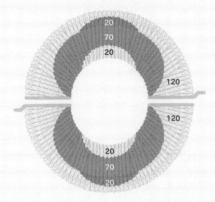

Wrap white yarn around the center first. Then, little by little, carefully cover the white yarn by wrapping pink yarn over it. By changing the color of yarn for this pattern, you can make many different flower designs.

Flowers –Small Pink Flower
(See p.8)
Type of Yarns: Fine – Lemon Yellow, White, Magenta, Yellow Green
Cardboard Template Width: 6cm/2.4in
Clover Pompom Maker: Small (Yellow, 1-5/8")

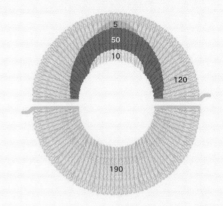

Using a pompom maker or a cardboard template, wrap white yarn around the center. Then wrap magenta yarn to cover the white. Wrap a small spot of yellow-green yarn before finally wrapping your lemon yellow yarn.

Flowers – Red and Pink
(See p.9)
Type of Yarns: Fine – Dark Yellow, Orange, Red, Pink, Green, Light Blue, Light Pink
Cardboard Template Width: 6cm/2.4in
Clover Pompom Maker: Small (Yellow, 1-5/8")

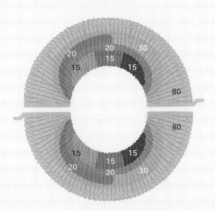

Using a pompom maker or a cardboard template. Wrap orange yarn around the center and then wrap dark yellow and red next to the orange. Wrap pink yarn so that it covers the first three yarns. Wrap green yarn to make a leaf by covering half of the pink yarn.

Flowers – White Petal Flower
(See p.10, leftmost)
Type of Yarns: Fine – Light Blue, Brown, White, Blue
Cardboard Template Width: 6cm/2.4in
Clover Pompom Maker: Small (Yellow, 1-5/8")

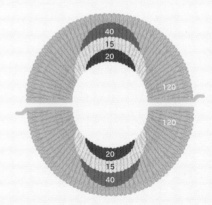

Wrap brown yarn around the center. Then wrap the white yarn to cover the brown. Next, wrap blue yarn around the center in a lump. Lastly, to make the flower design round, wrap the light blue yarn by pulling it toward the center as you go.

65

Fine - Various colors

Flowers – Blue Petal Flower
(See p.10, center)
Type of Yarns: Fine – Moss Green, Blue, Light Blue, White
Cardboard Template Width: 6cm/2.4in
Clover Pompom Maker: Small (Yellow, 1-5/8")

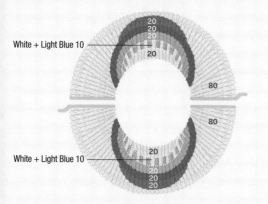

Wrap white yarn around the center. Next, hold the light blue and white together and wrap them as one. Next, wrap the light blue and then the blue yarn. Wrap moss green in a center lump. Lastly, wrap the white yarn. To make the flower round, pull towards the center as you go. Since many rounds are needed, you should wrap the yarn tightly to keep the design beautiful.

Flowers – Orange and Red Petal Flower
(See p.10, rightmost)
Type of Yarns: Fine – Orange, Red, Yellow Green, Green, White,
                        Light Blue, Light Pink
Cardboard Template Width: 6cm/2.4in
Clover Pompom Maker: Small (Yellow, 1-5/8")

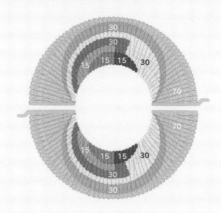

Using a pompom maker or a cardboard template, wrap orange and red yarn symmetrically around the center. Wrap yellow-green and green yarn to cover the orange. Wrap white, light blue and pink yarn so that you cover the wrapped yarn underneath.

Flowers – Mixed Pink Petal Flower
(See p.11, leftmost)
Type of Yarns: Fine – White / Light – Mint Green / Medium – Pink
Cardboard Template Width: 6cm/2.4in
Clover Pompom Maker: Small (Yellow, 1-5/8")

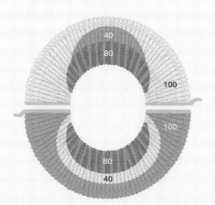

Wrap mixed pink yarn around the center. The design is different on the front and back, so use a pompom maker. On one arm, wrap white yarn to cover the mint green. On the other arm, first wrap white to completely cover the mixed pink, and then wrap mint green over the white. If you are using a template, use only the top or bottom half of the wrapping pattern (your flower will be the same color, front and back).

Flowers – Camellia
(See p.11, center)
Type of Yarns: Fine – Green, Moss Green, Yellow / Super Bulky – Red
Cardboard Template Width: 6cm/2.4in
Clover Pompom Maker: Small (Yellow, 1-5/8")

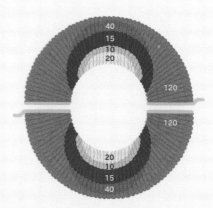

Wrap white yarn around the center and then wrap yellow to thinly cover it. Then, wrap the thick red yarn. Compactly wrap moss green around the center. Lastly, wrap green over everything. To make the flower design round, pull toward the center as you go.

Light - Mint Green   Medium - Mixed Pink   Super Bulky - Red

Flowers - Pink and White Poppy

(See p.11, right)
Type of Yarns: Fine – Brown, White, Pink, Green, Beige
Cardboard Template Width: 6cm/2.4in
Clover Pompom Maker: Small (Yellow, 1-5/8")

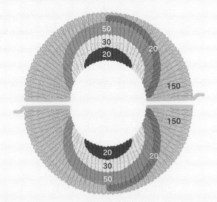

First wrap the brown, white, and pink yarns by successively covering the yarn wrapped underneath. Next, wrap green so that it covers about half of that underneath. Finally, wrap beige yarn over everything.

Flowers – Vermillion Petal

(See p.12)
Type of Yarns: Fine – Light Gray, Yellow, Vermillion, Dark Green
Cardboard Template Width: 6cm/2.4in
Clover Pompom Maker: Small (Yellow, 1-5/8")

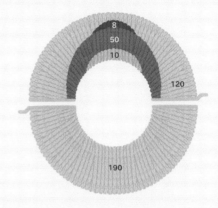

After wrapping yellow yarn, wrap vermillion to cover the yellow. Wrap dark green yarn as tightly to one spot as you can get it. Finally, wrap the light gray over everything.

Intricate Flowers – Carnation

(See p.13)
Type of Yarns: Fine – Light Pink, Salmon Pink, Red, Pink, Vermillion, Dark Green, Green, Yellow Green, Blue, White
Cardboard Template Width: 9cm/3.5in
Clover Pompom Maker: Large (Green, 2-1/2")

Type of Yarns: Fine – Magenta, Pink, Light Pink
Cardboard Template Width: 4cm/1.6in
Clover Pompom Maker: Small (Pink, 1-3/8")

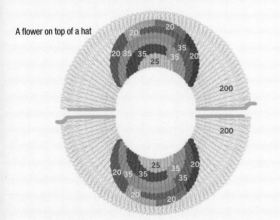

A flower on top of a hat

Magenta + Pink + Light Pink 150

Pompom attached to a hat

Magenta + Pink + Light Pink 150

Wrap light pink around the center. On top of that wrap red, salmon pink, pink, and vermillion, in that order, slightly overlapping each consecutive wrap at the center. For the leaves wrap three greens, then blue, over the other colors by dividing the circumference in quarters.

Take all three yarns at once and just wrap 50 rounds.

67

Intricate Flowers – Dahlia
(See p.16~17)
Type of Yarns: Fine – Yellow Green, Dark Red, Pink, White, Dark Yellow
Medium – Beige
Cardboard Template Width: 12cm/4.7in
Clover Pompom Maker: Large (Light Blue, 3-3/8")

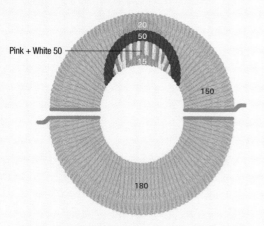

Pink + White 50

Flower Bouquets – Blue
(See p.14)
Type of Yarns: Fine – Moss Green, Blue, Light Blue, White
Cardboard Template Width: 9cm/3.5in
Clover Pompom Maker: Large (Green, 2-1/2")

Light Blue + White 20

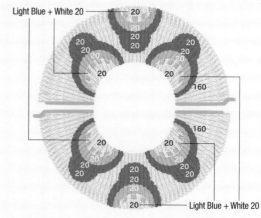

Light Blue + White 20

At first, wrap dark yellow and then, on top of that, wrap pink and white at the same time while holding the yarns together. Then, wrap dark red yarn to cover the wrapped pink and white yarn. Wrap yellow-green tight together in one spot and then wrap beige yarn to complete.

According to the wrapping pattern, carefully wrap the yarns in order. The wrapping method is the same as the Flower Bouquets – Small Pink Flowers (below left). To prevent the flower designs from touching and to make them come out beautiful wrap each yarn tightly.

Flower Bouquets – Small Pink Flowers
(See p.15, leftmost)
Type of Yarns: Fine – Brown, Magenta / Super Fine – Gold
Light – Green / Medium – Beige
Cardboard Template Width: 12cm/4.7in
Clover Pompom Maker: Large (Light Blue, 3-3/8")
Cardboard Template Width: 6cm/2.4in
Clover Pompom Maker: Small (Yellow, 1-5/8")

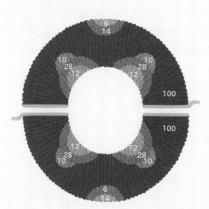

Flower Bouquets – Small Vermillion Flowers
(See p.15, second from left)
Type of Yarns: Fine – Light Blue, Vermillion, Blue, White
Cardboard Template Width: 6cm/2.4in
Clover Pompom Maker: Small (Yellow, 1-5/8")

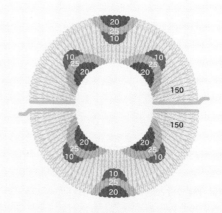

On top of gold yarn, wrap magenta. Then, wrap green around the center of the magenta. Make four of these, two on the top arm and two on the bottom. Then wrap brown yarn over top of everything. After you finish, make a dent in the outside center of the brown and wrap magenta and then gold yarn in this dent.

On top of vermillion yarn, wrap light blue. Wrap blue yarn around the center of the light blue yarn. Make four of these, two on the top arm and two on the bottom. Then wrap white yarn over top of everything. After finish wrapping make a large dent at the center and wrap blue, light blue, and vermillion yarn in the dent.

Medium - Beige   Super Fine - Gold   Light- Green

Flower Bouquets Yellow – Various Flowers

(See p.15, center)

Type of Yarns: Fine – White, Brown, Green, Off White, Pink, Navy Blue, Cream, Dark Green, Red, Light Pink

Cardboard Template Width: 6cm/2.4in

Clover Pompom Maker: Small (Yellow, 1-5/8")

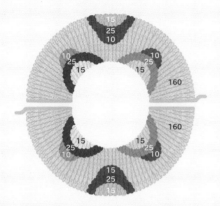

Wrap each flower part evenly in the following order – white → brown → green and then off-white → pink → navy blue. After you finish wrapping the cream yarn over everything make a dent in the center and wrap dark green, red, and light pink in the dent.

Flower Bouquets Black – Various Flowers

(See p.15, second from right)

Type of Yarns: Fine – White, Pink, Gray, Yellow, Orange, Yellow Green, Black, Red

Cardboard Template Width: 6cm/2.4in

Clover Pompom Maker: Small (Yellow, 1-5/8")

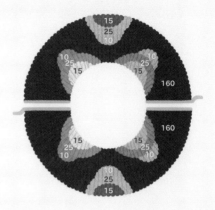

For this pompom use the same instructions as for Flower Bouquets Yellow– Various Flowers (on the left). Only the yarn colors are different.

Flower Bouquets Blue Green – Various Flowers

(See p.15, far right)

Type of Yarns: Fine – Dark Red, Black, White
Light – Blue Green

Cardboard Template Width: 6cm/2.4in

Clover Pompom Maker: Small (Yellow, 1-5/8")

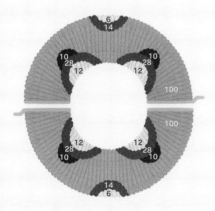

For this pompom use the same instructions as for Flower Bouquets – Small Pink Flowers on page 68. Use the specified colors of yarn.

Joined Yellow Pompoms – Pink Flowers

(See p.24)

Type of Yarns: Fine – Yellow, White, Pink, Salmon Pink, Red, Green, Yellow Green, Dark Yellow, Cream

Cardboard Template Width: 4cm/1.6in

Clover Pompom Maker: Small (Pink, 1-3/8")

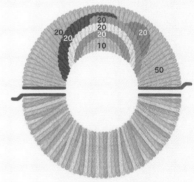

Yellow + Dark Yellow + Cream 150

Wrap yellow yarn around the center and wrap the other yarns over the yellow. After finishing one pompom tie a long strand of yarn at the side of the pompom, as instructed on page 59. Join two other pompoms afterward and then trim all at once.

69

Light - Blue Green

Joined Blue Pompoms – Pink Flowers

(See p.25)
Type of Yarns: Fine – Red, Pink, Moss Green, Yellow Green, White,
Light Blue
Cardboard Template Width: 4cm/1.6in
Clover Pompom Maker: Small (Pink, 1-3/8")

Pompoms on
Both Ends

20   35   40
15   15
50
180

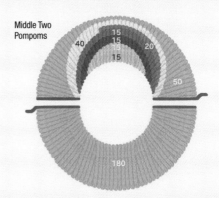

Type of Yarns: Fine – Yellow, Red, Light Pink, Moss Green, Green, White,
Light Blue
Cardboard Template Width: 4cm/1.6in
Clover Pompom Maker: Small (Pink, 1-3/8")

Middle Two
Pompoms

15
15
40   15   20
15
50
180

Wrap red and pink yarn evenly. Wrap yellow-green so it covers the red and pink. Next, wrap moss green to cover half of the yellow-green, then wrap white. Light blue covers everything underneath. Refer to page 59 for how to tie the strand that joins pompoms. Make the fourth pompom as per above. (The middle two pompoms are described next)

Wrap yellow yarn around the center. Cover the yellow yarn with light pink, red, and moss green yarn. Wrap green to cover half of the moss green. Wrap white to cover everything underneath. Lastly, wrap light blue yarn over everything and tie at the center. Make two more of these pompoms and join them to the first pompom made using the instructions above. Finally, add the forth pompom made using the instructions above.

Flowers with a Stem – Pink Petals

(See p.22, leftmost)
Type of Yarns: Fine – Brown, Light Pink, Magenta, Green, Blue, Gray
Cardboard Template Width: 6cm/2.4in
Clover Pompom Maker: Small (Yellow, 1-5/8")

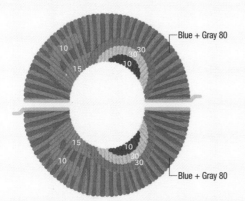

— Blue + Gray 80

10   30   30
15   10
15   10
10   30   30

— Blue + Gray 80

First, to create the stem, wrap 15 rounds of green yarn without overlapping. Next, wrap yarns according to the pattern to make a flower. Then, on top of the stem part, wrap one line of blue and gray yarn together. Wrap 10 rounds of green on top of this to make the leaf. At last, wrap blue and gray yarns together to cover everything.

Flowers with a Stem – Purple and Pink Petals

(See p.22, second from left)
Type of Yarns: Fine – Yellow, Purple, Pink, Navy Blue, Green, Beige
Cardboard Template Width: 6cm/2.4in
Clover Pompom Maker: Small (Yellow, 1-5/8")

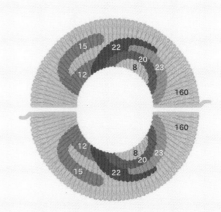

15   22   20   23
12   8
160
12   8   23
20
15   22
160

This is a variation of Flowers with a Stem – Pink Petals above. The instructions are almost the same. At first, to make the stem, wrap 12 rounds of green yarn in a single row without overlapping. Next, wrap yarns according to the pattern to make the flower. Then, on top of the stem part, wrap one round of beige yarn. Wrap 15 rounds of green in a single row, on top of the beige, to form the leaf. Last, cover everything in beige.

Flowers with a Stem – Blue and Yellow Petals

(See p.22, third from left)
Type of Yarns: Fine – White, Blue, Yellow, Light Blue, Gray, Brown
Cardboard Template Width: 9cm/3.5in
Clover Pompom Maker: Large (Green, 2-1/2")

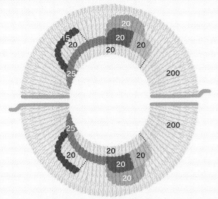

First, wrap the white yarn that comes between the flowers. Wrap 20 rounds to cover about 1/3 of the template's center. Next, from the opposite side, wrap a thin layer of gray to make a stem until the grey touches the white. Wrap the blue, yellow, and light blue and 2 rows of white to form the middle of the stem part. On top of that, wrap brown to make a leaf. Lastly, wrap white yarn over it all.

Flowers with a Stem – White and Pink Petals

(See p.23, leftmost)
Type of Yarns: Fine – Brown, Salmon Pink, White, Gray, Red
Cardboard Template Width: 6cm/2.4in
Clover Pompom Maker: Small (Yellow, 1-5/8")

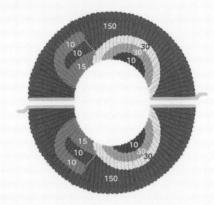

This pompom is the same as Flowers with a Stem – Pink Petals on page 70. First, wrap 15 rounds of gray to make a stem without overlapping. Next, wrap yarns according to the pattern to make the flowers. Then, on top of the stem, wrap a row of red and 10 rounds of gray in single row for the leaf. Lastly, wrap red over everything.

Flowers with a Stem – White and Mixed Pink Petals

(See p.23, third from right)
Type of Yarns: Fine – White / Light – Mint Green / Medium– Mixed Pink
Cardboard Template Width: 9cm/3.5in
Clover Pompom Maker: Large (Green, 2-1/2")

At first, wrap the mixed pink yarn. Wrap white for the leaf and the outside portion of the flower. Next, wrap mint green between the stem and the flower and then overlapping that wrap white for the stem of a second flower branching from the side. Wrap mixed pink yarn for the flower petal and then white for the outside of the petal. Lastly, wrap mint green over everything.

Flowers with a Stem – Yellow and Orange Petals

(See p.23, second from right)
Type of Yarns: Fine – Lemon Yellow, Orange, Yellow Green, White
Cardboard Template Width: 9cm/3.5in
Clover Pompom Maker: Large (Green, 2-1/2")

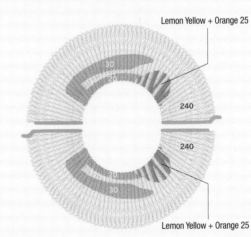

Lemon Yellow + Orange 25

Lemon Yellow + Orange 25

Hold yellow and orange yarns together closely and wrap them at the same time. Wrap 20 rounds of yellow-green yarn in a single row. Wrap white yarn on top of that to form a part of the stem and then wrap yellow-green for an external leaf.

Light - Mint Green   Medium - Mixed Pink

Flowers with a Stem –
Red and Yellow Petals

(See p.23, rightmost)
Type of Yarns: Super Bulky – White, Red / Super Bulky – Yellow, Gray
Cardboard Template Width: 12cm/4.7in
Clover Pompom Maker: Large (Light Blue, 3-3/8")

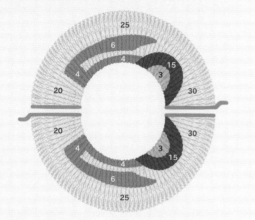

It makes it easier if you wrap 20 rounds of white on the left first and then wrap yellow. Thick yarn is used for this pompom so wrap it tight. The number of rounds is small so that make it relatively easy.

Semicircular Pompoms –
Pink Flower

(See p.26, top)
Type of Yarns: Fine – White, Moss Green, Light Pink, Pink, Yellow Green
Light – Navy Blue / Super Fine – Gold
Cardboard Template Width: 4.5cm/1.8in
Clover Pompom Maker: Large (Green, 2-1/2")

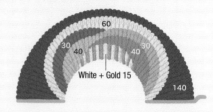

Except for the petals, wrap yarns to overlap alternatively for leaves. This makes the pompom look intricate. After removing the template or pompom maker, attach a piece of felt for easier trimming (see p.62). Even lightly trimmed, this pompom looks gorgeous and is relatively easy to make.

Semicircular Pompoms –
Flowers with a Stem

(See p.26, bottom)
Type of Yarns: Fine – White, Pink, Red, Yellow, Orange,
Moss Green, Green
Cardboard Template Width: 4.5cm/1.8in
Clover Pompom Maker: Large (Green, 2-1/2")

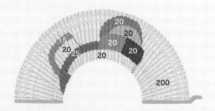

Use one arm of the pompom maker. First, wrap 20 rounds of white over 1/3 of the template's center. This white will be between the flower pattern. Next, from the opposite side, start wrapping a thin layer of moss green until it touches the white to make the stem. Wrap pink, red, yellow, and orange and then wrap about 2 rows of white from the middle of the stem. On top of that, wrap green yarn to make a leaf. Lastly, wrap white over everything.

Semicircular Pompoms –
Pompom Brooch

(See p.27)
Type of Yarns: Fine – Brown, Light Pink, White, Pink, Red, Green,
Moss Green, Dark Green, Yellow Green
Cardboard Template Width: 4.5cm/1.8in
Clover Pompom Maker: Large (Green, 2-1/2")

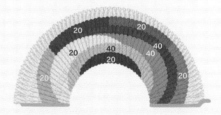

Use one arm of the pompom maker. First, wrap brown at the center and then wrap light pink to cover the brown. Next, wrap white a little over halfway down the arm and pink to overlap the white at the center. Do the same for red yarn. Then wrap each shade of green over top and, lastly, wrap white over everything.

Super Bulky - White/Red   Super Bulky - Yellow/Gray   Light - Navy-blue   Super Fine - Gold

Semicircular Pompoms – Pink
(See p.27)
Type of Yarns: Fine – Magenta, Pink, Light Pink
Cardboard Template Width: 4cm/1.8in
Clover Pompom Maker: Small (Pink, 1-3/8")

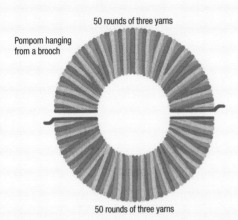

50 rounds of three yarns

Pompom hanging from a brooch

50 rounds of three yarns

This round pompom hangs from a semicircular pompom brooch. Simply wrap 50 rounds of all three yarns at same time. Cut about 1m/39 inches of each yarn and bundle them together. Tie the center of the pompom with this bundle then braid the trailing ends. Use the braided strands to attach the pompom to the semicircular pompom that forms the body of the brooch.

(See p.33)
Type of Yarns: Fine – White, Navy Blue / Super Fine – Gold
Cardboard Template Width: 2cm/0.8in
Clover Pompom Maker: X-Small (Purple, 1")

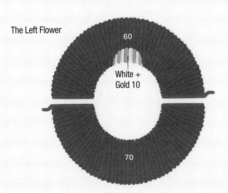

The Left Flower

60

White + Gold 10

70

When using a pompom maker, wrap the yarns according to the wrapping pattern. If you use a cardboard template, make a pompom using only top half of the wrapping pattern. Tie the center with both a strand of yarn and a floral wire and wrap floral tape around the whole.

Corsages
(See p.33)
Type of Yarns: Fine – White, Blue, Navy Blue
Cardboard Template Width: 4cm/1.8in
Clover Pompom Maker: Small (Pink, 1-3/8")

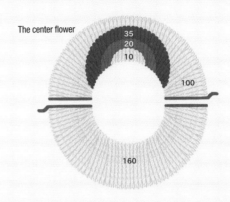

The center flower

35
20
10

100

160

Start by wrapping white yarn at the center. Cover each consecutive layer as you go. After you finish, tie the center with a strand of yarn. Use a thin floral wire (used for art flowers) to tie the center again and wrap the trailing strands around the wire to make one string. Wrap floral tape around the string. Bundle this with the two pompoms shown below and secure everything with floral tape. Complete with a brooch pin.

(See p.33)
Type of Yarns: Fine – Dark Yellow, Brown
Cardboard Template Width: 2cm/0.8in
Clover Pompom Maker: X-Small (Purple, 1")

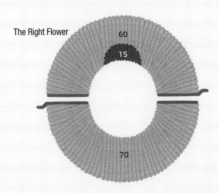

The Right Flower

60

15

70

With a pompom maker, wrap yarn according to the pattern. With a template, make a pompom using only the top half of the pattern. Tie the center with both a strand of yarn and a floral wire and then put floral tape around the whole.

*Use the same instructions for Corsages on page 32. Use different colors of yarn and give it a try.

73

Medal – Light Blue and White
(See p.30, top right)
Type of Yarns: Fine – Light Blue, White
Cardboard Template Width: 6cm/2.4in
Clover Pompom Maker: Small (Yellow, 1-5/8")

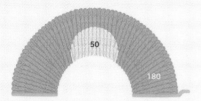

Wrap white yarn tightly at the center. This is a semicircular pompom so attaching a piece of felt to the back makes trimming easier (see p.62). Make the piece of felt small. See below for attaching the ribbon.

Medal – Red and White
(See p.30, top left)
Type of Yarns: Fine – Red, White
Cardboard Template Width: 6cm/2.4in
Clover Pompom Maker: Small (Yellow, 1-5/8")

When you remove the template or pompom maker after wrapping the yarn, make sure the white yarn does not gather at the center. Trim the pompom so that the white yarn is visible on the back side. See below for attaching a ribbon.

Medal – Green and White
(See p.30, bottom right)
Type of Yarns: Fine – Green, White
Cardboard Template Width: 6cm/2.4in
Clover Pompom Maker: Small (Yellow, 1-5/8")

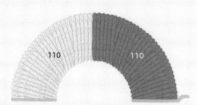

Wrap the yarn tight so that it does not shift around. See below for attaching a ribbon.

Medal – Brown, Pink and White
(See p.30, bottom left)
Type of Yarns: Fine – Brown, Pink, White
Cardboard Template Width: 6cm/2.4in
Clover Pompom Maker: Small (Yellow, 1-5/8")

Pay attention to the wrapping position of the white and pink yarns that make the center of the pompom. Wrap the brown yarn so that it is evenly distributed on each side of the pink and white. See below for attaching a ribbon.

Fold a piece of ribbon in half and tuck the corners under. Sew them to secure temporarily. Place and sew a pin across the top, on one side of the folded ribbon.

If you want to double the ribbon, place another ribbon over the first and secure it.

Insert the ribbon in between the pompom and felt and sew together.

Simple Stripes

(See p.20)
Type of Yarns: Fine – Light Blue, White
Cardboard Template Width: 12cm/1.7in
Clover Pompom Maker: Large (Light Blue, 3-3/8")

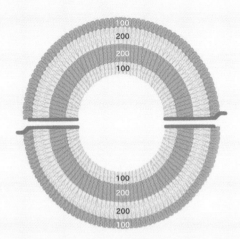

Wrap yarn carefully, in order, according to the wrapping pattern. Since the first and last wrappings will roughly double in size after removing the cardboard template or pompom maker. To make sure that the stripes are evenly distributed there are only half the number of wraps on the inside and the outside, as per the pattern.

Stripes in Variations - Multicolored

(See p.21, leftmost)
Type of Yarns: Fine – Green, Yellow, Pink, White, Dark Yellow, Light Blue
Cardboard Template Width: 12cm/4.7in
Clover Pompom Maker: Large (Light Blue, 3-3/8")

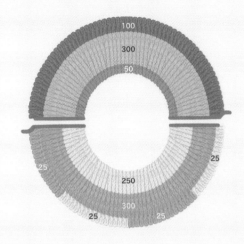

By changing the number of rounds and the yarns you can make a really free-feeling pompom like this one. Not wrapping the yarn evenly makes an interesting pompom like this.

Stripes in Variations – Red, White and Blue

(See p.21, second from left)
Type of Yarns: Fine – Navy Blue, White, Red
Cardboard Template Width: 4cm/1.6in
Clover Pompom Maker: Small (Pink, 1-3/8")

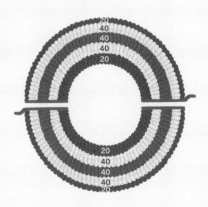

Try to wrap each yarn even in thickness. Fix the stripes using the tip of your scissors as you trim in order to make it truly beautiful.

Stripes in Variations – Pink, White and Gray

(See p.21, second from right)
Type of Yarns: Fine – Gray, Pink, White
Cardboard Template Width: 6cm/2.4in
Clover Pompom Maker: Small (Yellow, 1-5/8")

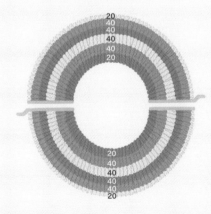

Try to wrap each yarn even in thickness. Fix the stripes using the tip of your scissors as you trim in order to make it truly beautiful.

Stripes in Variations – Pink, Ocher and Red

(See p.21, rightmost)
Type of Yarns: Medium – Pink, Ocher, Red
Cardboard Template Width: 9cm/3.5in
Clover Pompom Maker: Large (Green, 2-1/2")

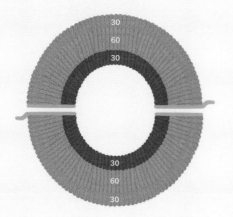

Wrap the thick yarn tightly. After removing the cardboard template or pompom maker, the first and last yarn that you wrapped will double in size so, to make the stripes even, we have reduced the number of rounds by half.

Butterfly

(See p.06)
Type of Yarns: Fine – Yellow, Light Blue, Dark Green
Cardboard Template Width: 3cm/1.2in
Clover Pompom Maker: Small (Yellow, 1-5/8")

Detailed instructions are on page 61. All the Butterfly pompoms on page 6 use the same instructions but different colors of yarn. Use the same yarn for the wings and antenna if you want them to be the same color.

Scarf

(See p.42)
Type of Yarns: Bulky – Pink / Medium – Yellow
Cardboard Template Width: 9cm/3.5in
Clover Pompom Maker: Large (Green, 2-1/2")

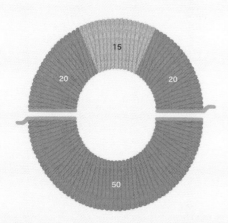

After you tie the center of the first pompom, be sure to tie a long strand of yarn (longer than the scarf) in a different direction (see page 59). Then join 12 to 13 (or the desired number) pompoms together. Tie a hair-elastic on the end to complete. When you wear the scarf, hook the hair elastic to the pompom on the opposite end.

Bear Scarf – Body

(See p.43)
Type of Yarns: Bulky – White, Beige
Cardboard Template Width: 9cm/3.5in
Clover Pompom Maker: Large (Green, 2-1/2")

* Prepare buttons for the eyes.

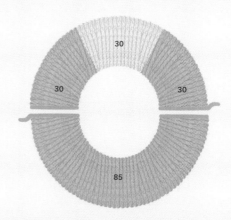

Use the same instruction as for the pink scarf above to make the bear's body. After that, make the face of the bear (on the next page) and attach it to the body.

Medium - Pink/Ocher/Red/Yellow   Bulky - Pink   Bulky - White

Bear Scarf – Face

(See p.43)

Type of Yarns: Fine – Brown, White, Black

[Ears and Nose]
Cardboard Template Width: 4cm/1.6in
Clover Pompom Maker: Small (Pink, 1-3/8")

[Face]
Cardboard Template Width: 6cm/2.4in
Clover Pompom Maker: Small (Yellow, 1-5/8")

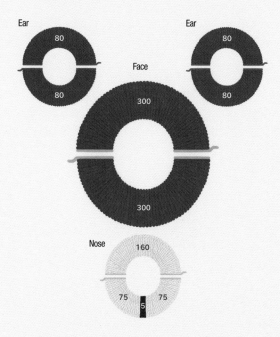

Make pompoms for each of the ears, the face, and the nose (the pompom for nose should be tied with brown yarn). Use the trailing strings from the center of each pompom, attach and secure them on the "body" of the scarf made on page 76. Attach any type of eyes that you want in order to complete.

Bunny Bracelet

(See p.43)

Type of Yarns: Fine – White, Black

[Face]
Cardboard Template Width: 9cm/3.5in
Clover Pompom Maker: Large (Green, 2-1/2")

[Ears]
Cardboard Template Width: 4cm/1.6in
Clover Pompom Maker: Small (Pink, 1-3/8")

[Nose]
Cardboard Template Width: 6cm/2.4in
Clover Pompom Maker: Small (Yellow, 1-5/8")

* Prepare buttons and other materials that you wish for eyes.

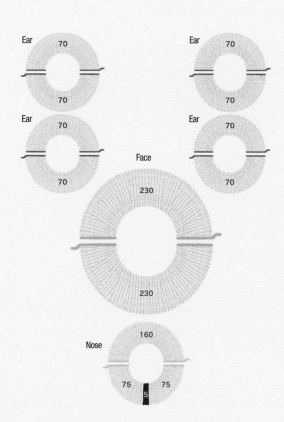

Make pompoms for each of the ears, the face, and the nose (the pompom for nose should be tied with brown yarn). Use the trailing strings from the center of each pompom, attach and secure them on the "body" of the scarf made on page 76. Attach any type of eyes that you want in order to complete.

Bulky - Beige

Wreath

(See p.36)

Type of Yarns: Fine – Gray / Medium – Red, Dark Red, White
              Light – Mixed Pink
Cardboard Template Width: 4cm/1.6in
Clover Pompom Maker: Small (Pink, 1-3/8")

* Make four red, two dark red, three white, two pink, one gray, and two mixed
  color pompoms.

Decoration – Small

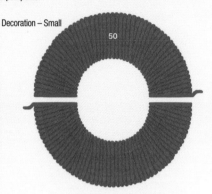

For red and white yarn, wrap 50 rounds.
For gray and mixed pink, wrap 180 rounds.

Type of Yarns: Fine – Gray / Medium – Red, Dark Red
Cardboard Template Width: 6cm/2.4in
Clover Pompom Maker: Small (Yellow, 1-5/8")

* Make two red, one dark red, one gray.

Decoration – Medium

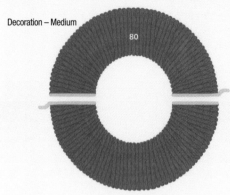

For red wrap 80 rounds.
For gray 240 rounds.

Type of Yarns: Medium – Off White, Light Green, Dark Green,
                    Moss Green

Cardboard Template Width: 9cm/3.5in

Clover Pompom Maker: Large (Green, 2-1/2")

Light Green + Moss Green 130

Body – Small

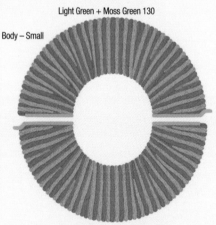

130 rounds for each pompom

* Make two pompoms for each
Using off white and light green together / Using light green and moss green together
Using moss green and dark green together / Using moss green

Make each part according to the pattern. Then, stick a wire through the
pompoms that make the wreath body (small and large). Sticking a wire
through a center of the pompom prevents it from becoming disheveled.
Twist the wire at the top and make a loop to hang the wreath. Wire
decoration pompoms to the wreath. Use glue, or a string, to attach
golden decorations. Affix a ribbon to the loop for hanging the wreath.

Type of Yarns: Medium – Dark Green
Cardboard Template Width: 12cm/4.7in
Clover Pompom Maker: Large (Light Blue, 3-3/8")

* Make five dark green pompoms.

Body – Large

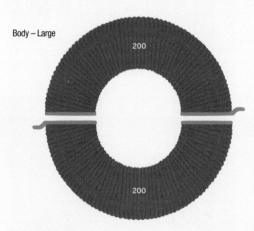

Gold Decoration
Decorations used for making wreaths, etc.
Bundle forty pieces together and tie them in the middle. Make five sets.

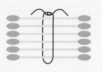

The gold decoration is a ready-made
article often used for wreaths.
Bundle about forty pieces and tie the
bundle together in the middle using
a string.

78

Medium - Red, Dark Red, White, Off White, Light Green, Dark Green, Moss Green

Snowman

(See p.37)
Type of Yarns: Fine – Red
Cardboard Template Width: 4cm/1.6in
Clover Pompom Maker: Small (Pink, 1 -3/8")

Type of Yarns: Fine – White, Black, Orange
Cardboard Template Width: 6cm/2.4in
Clover Pompom Maker: Small (Yellow, 1-5/8")

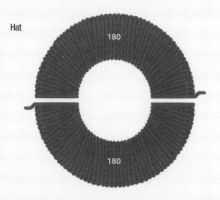

Hat

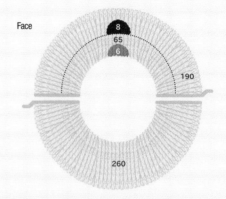

Face

After removing the template or pompom maker, trim the pompom into a hat. It is best to make the face now as well so the size of hat and face match. Leave the strand of yarn used to tie the pompom at the center a little long. Thread the trailing yarn through a yarn needle and push that through the center of the face. Tie in place.

Similar to the hat, leave the strand of yarn used tie the pompom at the center a little bit long. Thread the trailing strand of yarn through a yarn needle and push it through the center of the trimmed body. Tie it in place.

Type of Yarns: Fine – Red, Light Blue / Lace – Gold
Cardboard Template Width: 9cm/3.5in
Clover Pompom Maker: Large (Green, 2-1/2")

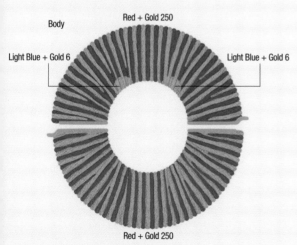

Body

Red + Gold 250

Light Blue + Gold 6

Light Blue + Gold 6

Red + Gold 250

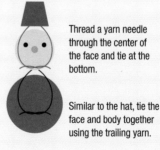

Thread a yarn needle through the center of the face and tie at the bottom.

Similar to the hat, tie the face and body together using the trailing yarn.

Hold and wrap red yarn (for the green snowman on p. 37, use green yarn) and gold yarn at same time. After making each part, join the hat, face and body together.

Light - Mixed Pink   Lace - Gold

Christmas Tree Ornament –
Flower with Four Petals
(See p.38, top left)
Type of Yarns: Fine – Yellow / Light – Light Green / White, Pink
Cardboard Template Width: 6cm/2.4in
Clover Pompom Maker: Small (Yellow, 1-5/8")

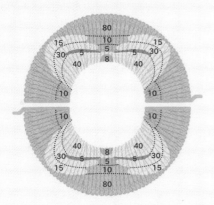

First, wrap light green yarn on each side to hold the flower pattern in place. Next, wrap yellow at the center. Wrap 40 rounds of white and then over that, from the middle, start wrapping pink yarn towards the yellow. First, wrap 30 rounds of white on the left, then 5 rounds of light green in the middle. Finally, wrap white yarn on the right. Continue piling the correct number of rounds on top of each successive layer. Lastly, wrap light green over everything.

Christmas Tree Ornament –
Gray Polka Dots
(See p.38, bottom right)
Type of Yarns: Super Bulky – Gray, White
Cardboard Template Width: 9cm/3.5in
Clover Pompom Maker: Large (Green, 2-1/2")

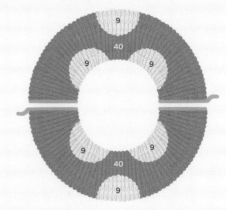

Very thick yarn is used here so wrap the yarn tightly to help it stay put. The number of rounds is less so that it can be made in a relatively small amount of time.

Christmas Tree Ornament –
Pink Polka Dots
(See p.38, bottom center)
Type of Yarns: Super Bulky – Pink, Yellow
Cardboard Template Width: 9cm/3.5in
Clover Pompom Maker: Large (Green, 2-1/2")

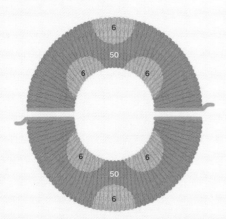

This is the same polka dot pompom as the top left, but in a different color. Very thick yarn is used here so wrap the yarn tightly to help it stay on. There are fewer rounds in this pompom so it can be made in a relatively small amount of time.

Christmas Tree Ornament – Colorful
(See p.38, bottom left)
Type of Yarns: Fine – White, Yellow, Light Blue, Yellow Green, Pink
Light – Mixed Pink / Super Fine – Gold
Cardboard Template Width: 9cm/3.5in
Clover Pompom Maker: Large (Green, 2-1/2")

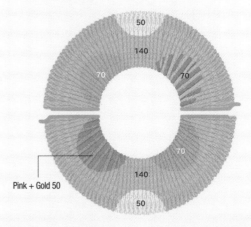

Pink + Gold 50

This is the same polka dot pompom as above just in a different color yarn. Simply changing the color of yarn makes the aesthetic of the pompom different. You can enjoy many different combinations of yarn and making great-looking pompoms.

Light - Light Green   Light - White/Pink   Super Bulky - Gray/Pink/Yellow

Candles

(See p.39)

Type of Yarns: Fine – Beige, Yellow, Orange, Dark Red, Red, Gray
Lace – Silver

Cardboard Template Width: 12cm/4.7in

Clover Pompom Maker: Large (Light Blue, 3-3/8")

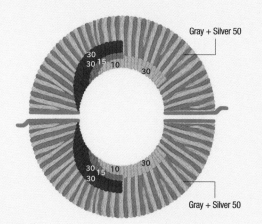

Gray + Silver 50

30
30 15 10 30

30 10 30
15
30

Gray + Silver 50

Wrap the yarn according to the pattern. To make the gradation of flame beautiful, adjust the yarn using the tip of your scissors as you trim.

Angels

(See p.39)

Type of Yarns: Fine – White, Navy Blue, Gray / Lace – Gold
Super Fine – Gold

Cardboard Template Width: 9cm/3.5in

Clover Pompom Maker: Large (Green, 2-1/2")

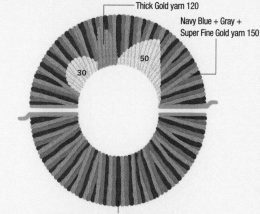

Thick Gold yarn 120

Navy Blue + Gray + Super Fine Gold yarn 150

30   50

Navy Blue + Gray + Super Fine Gold yarn 230

Wrap the yarn according to the pattern. To place the gold wing in between the head and body, adjust the yarn using the tip of your scissors as you trim.

Earrings

(See p.40)

Type of Yarns: Fine – Magenta / Super Fine – Gold

Cardboard Template Width: 2cm/0.8in

Clover Pompom Maker: X-Small (Purple, 1")

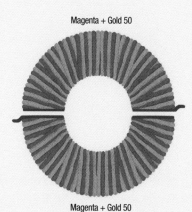

Magenta + Gold 50

Magenta + Gold 50

Wrap pink and gold yarn together for this pompom. Tie the center with pink yarn. Before removing the pompom maker (or template), bundle five long gold threads together and tie them at the center of the pompom. Trim gold threads to length. Secure the pompom to an earring hoop using the pink center-tied yarn.

Super Bulky - White   Knife Angela - Mixed Pink   Lace - Silver/Gold   Super Fine - Gold

Necklaces

(See p.41)

Type of Yarns: Fine – Yellow, White, Yellow Green, Magenta, Dark Yellow, Gray,
Light Pink, Light Blue, Lemon Yellow

Cardboard Template Width: 6cm/2.4in

Clover Pompom Maker: Small (Yellow, 1-5/8")

Cardboard Template Width: 2cm/0.8in

Clover Pompom Maker: X-Small (Purple, 1")

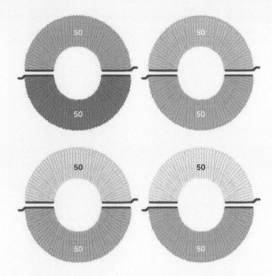

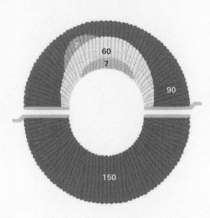

For smaller pompoms change the colors on each side (when using a cardboard template, wrap different colors on the right and left.) Lightly trim the pompoms and make them look somewhat disheveled. Lastly, attach pompoms on a necklace base using the yarn tied around the center (bird-shaped lace string was used here).

Multicolored 1-1

(See p.4)

Type of Yarns: Fine – Black, Yellow, Green

Cardboard Template Width: 6cm/2.4in

Clover Pompom Maker: Small (Yellow, 1-5/8")

Combine three strands of black yarn,
one of yellow and one of green, 40 rounds.

Combine three strands of black yarn,
one of yellow and one of green, 40 rounds.

Bundle three strands of black yarn, one strand of yellow, and one of green together, then wrap 40 rounds of all five strands around your pompom maker or template.

Multicolored 1-2

(See p.4)

Type of Yarns: Light – Light Blue, Pink

Cardboard Template Width: 6cm/2.4in

Clover Pompom Maker: Small (Yellow, 1-5/8"))

Combine two yarns together – 100 rounds.

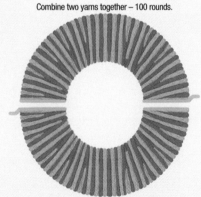

Combine two yarns together – 100 rounds.

Bundle the two yarns together and wrap 100 rounds with both strands at the same time.

Light - Light Blue   Light - Pink

Multicolored 1-3

(See p.4)

Type of Yarns: Fine – Dark Yellow, Red, Pink, Light Purple,
Light Blue, Yellow Green, Blue Green
Cardboard Template Width: 6cm/2.4in
Clover Pompom Maker: Small (Yellow, 1-5/8")

Combine seven yarns together – 28 rounds.

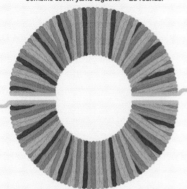

Combine seven yarns together – 28 rounds.

Bundle seven yarns together and wrap 28 rounds with all seven strands
of yarn at the same time.

Multicolored 1-4

(See p.4)

Type of Yarns: Fine – Navy Blue, Dark Red / Lace – Silver
Cardboard Template Width: 4cm/1.6in
Clover Pompom Maker: Small (Pink, 1-3/8")

Combine three yarns together – 70 rounds.

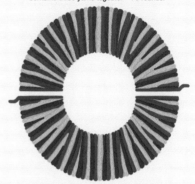

Combine three yarns together – 70 rounds.

Bundle three yarns together and wrap 70 rounds with all three strands
of yarn at the same time.

Multicolored 1-5

(See p.4)

Type of Yarns: Fine – Dark Yellow, Yellow, Cream
Cardboard Template Width: 4cm/1.6in
Clover Pompom Maker: Small (Pink, 1-3/8")

Combine three yarns together – 50 rounds.

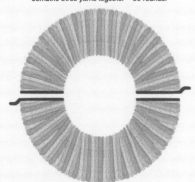

Combine three yarns together – 50 rounds.

Bundle three yarns together and wrap 50 rounds with all three strands
of yarn at the same time.

Multicolored 1-6

(See p.5)

Type of Yarns: Fine – Light Blue, Navy Blue, Yellow Green, Green, Dark Green
Light – Blue Green
Cardboard Template Width: 9cm/3.5in
Clover Pompom Maker: Large (Green, 2-1/2")

Combine six yarns together – 50 rounds.

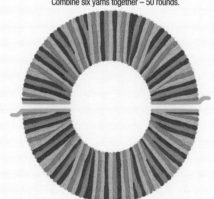

Combine six yarns together – 50 rounds.

Bundle six yarns together and wrap 50 rounds with all three strands of
yarn at the same time.

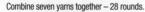

Lace - Silver   Light - Blue Green

Multicolored 2-2

(See p.5)
Type of Yarns: Fine – Dark Red
                Light – Blue Green, Green
Cardboard Template Width: 6cm/2.4in
Clover Pompom Maker: Small (Yellow, 1-5/8")

Combine two strands of blue-green, two strands of green, and one strand of dark red yarn together – 40 rounds.

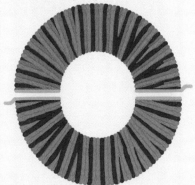

Combine four strands of blue-green, and one strand of dark red yarn together – 40 rounds.

Bundle two strands of blue-green, two of green, and one strand of dark red together. Wrap 40 rounds with all five strands of yarn at the same time. On the other arm, bundle four strands of blue-green yarn and one strand of dark red. Wrap 40 rounds with all five strands of yarn. For a template, wrap one bundle on the right half and the other bundle on left half.

Multicolored 2-3

(See p.5)
Type of Yarns: Fine – Brown
                Light – Mint Green
Cardboard Template Width: 4cm/1.6in
Clover Pompom Maker: Small (Pink, 1-3/8")

Combine the yarns together – 70 rounds.

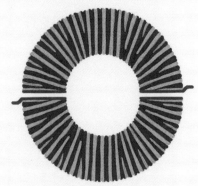

Combine the yarns together – 70 rounds.

Bundle the yarns together and wrap 70 rounds with both yarns at the same time.

Multicolored 2-4

(See p.5)
Type of Yarns: Fine – Cream, Yellow Green, Salmon Pink
Cardboard Template Width: 6cm/2.4in
Clover Pompom Maker: Small (Yellow, 1-5/8")

Combine the three yarns together – 50 rounds.

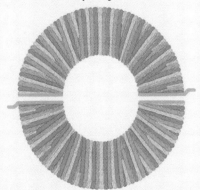

Combine the three yarns together – 50 rounds.

Bundle all three yarns together and wrap 50 rounds with them at the same time.

Multicolored 2-5

(See p.5)
Type of Yarns: Fine – Light Pink, Light Blue, White
Cardboard Template Width: 4cm/1.6in
Clover Pompom Maker: Small (Pink, 1-3/8")

Combine the three yarns together – 50 rounds.

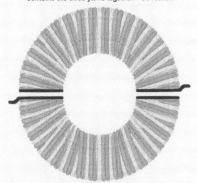

Combine the three yarns together – 50 rounds.

Bundle three yarns together and wrap 50 rounds with them at the same time.

Light - Blue Green/Green/Mint Green

Multicolored 2-6

(See p.5)
Type of Yarns: Fine – Magenta, Pink, Light Pink
Cardboard Template Width: 4cm/1.6in
Clover Pompom Maker: Small (Pink, 1-3/8")

Combine three yarns
together – 50 rounds.

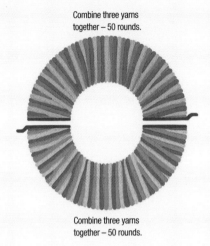

Combine three yarns
together – 50 rounds.

Bundle three yarns together and wrap 50 rounds with them at the same time.

Scenery – Night Sky

(See p.28 left)
Type of Yarns: Super Fine – Silver / Fine – White / Light – Navy Blue
Cardboard Template Width: 12cm/4.7in
Clover Pompom Maker: Large (Light Blue, 3-3/8")

All the round dots =
2 rounds of white and silver

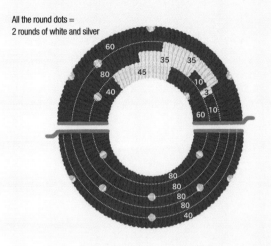

Dividing and wrapping the pattern in layers is easiest. Between the layers, wrap 2 rounds of white and silver yarn. After trimming, adjust the moon using the tip of your scissors. The front and back have a different pattern, so use a pompom maker. If you use a template, use either the top or bottom of the wrapping pattern to make a pompom and make the same pattern on both sides.

Scenery – Seagull

(See p.28 right)
Type of Yarns: Fine – Navy Blue, Light Blue, White, Black
Cardboard Template Width: 6cm/2.4in
Clover Pompom Maker: Small (Yellow, 1-5/8")

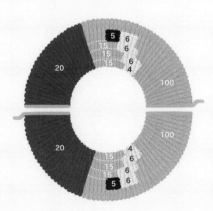

You might find it confusing to get the seagull shape in an arch, but if you wrap the light blue yarn a little bit wider at first and then wrap the white on top it helps make it arched.

Scenery – Tree

(See p.29 left)
Type of Yarns: Fine – White, Green, Gray, Brown
Cardboard Template Width: 12cm/4.7in
Clover Pompom Maker: Large (Light Blue, 3-3/8")

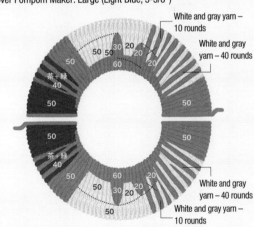

White and gray yarn –
10 rounds

White and gray
yarn – 40 rounds

White and gray
yarn – 40 rounds

White and gray yarn –
10 rounds

First, start wrapping the ground portion. Next, wrap 60 green rounds for the tree trunk and 50 white rounds on top. Wrap the yarn for leaves and the sky portions alternately (30, 20, 20) and then wrap 50 rounds of gray on the end. Wrap 40 rounds of white and gray bundled together then 50 rounds of white. While trimming, make the tree trunk portion and the tree's pointiness distinct so it is more treelike.

85

Super Fine - Silver   Light - Navy-blue

Scenery – Tree and House

(See p.29 right)
Type of Yarns: Fine – White, Light Blue, Brown, Red
Cardboard Template Width: 12cm/4.7in
Clover Pompom Maker: Large (Light Blue, 3-3/8")

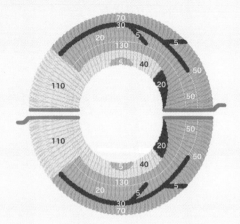

First, wrap 110 rounds of white snow. Next, wrap 5 rounds of light blue for a window, then white and red to make the house and roof. Wrap 130 rounds of light blue over the house. Next, wrap 20 rounds of light blue and 5 of brown on top. Leave a space about the width of a strand of yarn. Wrap 50 rounds of light blue in piles. Wrap 30 rounds of brown for a tree trunk and 50 rounds of light blue on the right. Add 5 rounds of brown to make a branch and 70 rounds of light blue over that.

Pink Droplets

(See p.18)
Type of Yarns: Super Fine – Gold / Fine – White / Medium – Pink
Cardboard Template Width: 12cm/4.7in
Clover Pompom Maker: Large (Light Blue, 3-3/8")

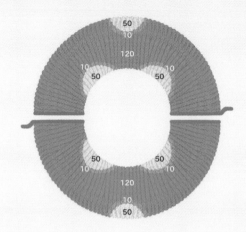

Since this is a water spot pattern, wrap the white yarn so it doesn't spread out too much. This will make beautiful spots. Insert pink yarn so that the water spots are not touching each other.

Colorful Ring Droplets

(See p.19 left)
Type of Yarns: Fine – White, Dark Yellow, Brown, Pink, Light Blue, Gray
Cardboard Template Width: 6cm/2.4in
Clover Pompom Maker: Small (Yellow, 1-5/8")

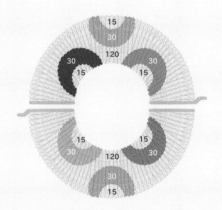

Wrap the yarn carefully in order to cover the layers underneath. This pompom seems complicated at first sight, but each color is separated and it is actually easy to adjust the droplets. Since the pattern is different on the top and bottom, use a pompom maker.

Black Droplets

(See p.19 center)
Type of Yarns: Fine – Black, Gray, White
Cardboard Template Width: 6cm/2.4in
Clover Pompom Maker: Small (Yellow, 1-5/8")

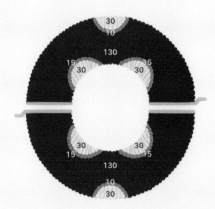

Since this is a water spot pattern, wrap the white yarn so it doesn't spread out too much. This makes for beautiful water spots. Insert black yarn so that the water spots are not touching each other.

Super Fine - Gold   Medium - Pink

Colorful Ring Droples

(See p.19 right)
Type of Yarns: Fine – White, Dark Yellow, Brown, Pink, Light Blue, Gray
Cardboard Template Width: 9cm/3.5in
Clover Pompom Maker: Large (Green, 2-1/2")

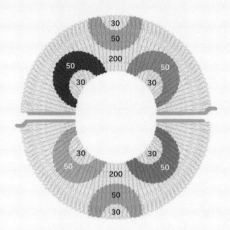

Carefully wrap yarn being sure to cover each consecutive layer. This pompom may seem complicated at first glance, but each color is separated and it is actually easy to adjust the droplets. Since the pattern is different on the top and bottom, use a pompom maker.

Matryoshka Doll – Small

(See p.44 left)
Type of Yarns: Fine – Dark Red, Tan, Brown, Black, Dark Yellow, Yellow

[Head]
Cardboard Template Width: 4cm/1.6in
Clover Pompom Maker: Small (Pink, 1-3/8")

[Body]
Cardboard Template Width: 6cm/2.4in
Clover Pompom Maker: Small (Yellow, 1-5/8")

For the head, wrap yarn according to the pattern. Leave the yarn used to tie the center a little bit long. After you finish wrapping body, join the head to the body (see p.59 for instructions.) Trim the pompom using scissors. Trim the pompom all over so it is smaller than a medium size pompom. Since the eyes, mouth, and hair are easily disheveled, adjust them with your scissors.

Tie the trailing strands of yarn to the body.

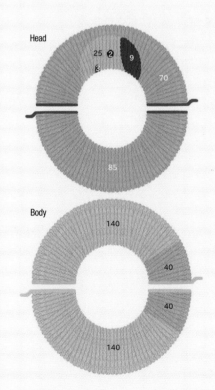

87

Matryoshka Doll – Medium

(See p.44 right)
Type of Yarns: Fine – Dark Red, Tan, Brown, Black, Dark Yellow, Yellow
                Light – Green
Cardboard Template Width: 6cm/2.4in
Clover Pompom Maker: Small (Yellow, 1-5/8")

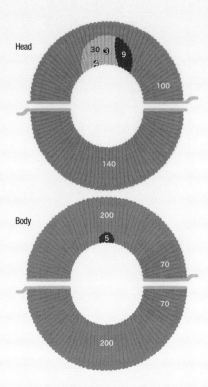

For the head wrap the yarn according to the pattern. Leave the yarn used to tie the center of the pompom a little bit long. After you finish wrapping the body, join the head to the body (see p.59 for instructions on joining). Trim the pompom using scissors. Adjust the pompom's shape as you trim. Make the head smaller than the body. The eyes, mouth, and hair easily become disheveled so be sure to adjust them using the tip of your scissors.

Matryoshka Doll – Large

(See p.45)
Type of Yarns: Fine – Dark Red, Tan, Brown, Black, Dark Yellow, Yellow
                Medium – Red / Light – Green, Blue Green

[Head]
Cardboard Template Width: 6cm/2.4in
Clover Pompom Maker: Small (Yellow, 1-5/8")

[Body]
Cardboard Template Width: 9cm/3.5in
Clover Pompom Maker: Large (Green, 2-1/2")

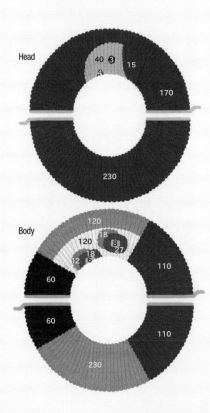

For the head, wrap yarn according to the pattern. For the flower patterns in the body, start wrapping the left center flower in the pattern first. Next, wrap white yarn to cover the flower pattern and wrap about 30 rounds of white yarn on the right side to make the surface flat. On top of this, wrap 12 rounds of red yarn then wrap yellow yarn to make the flower's center and wrap 15 rounds of red yarn to cover the yellow. Wrap green yarn to cover the left side of the red flower and then the flower pattern is done. Then, wrap white yarn over the flowers as per the pattern. The rest of the instructions are the same as for the Matryoshka Doll – Small on page 87.

Light - Green/Blue Green   Midium - Red

Hamburger

(See p.46)

Type of Yarns: Fine – Red Brown, Beige, Yellow, Brown, Yellow Green
Light – Light Brown, Ocher, Red

Cardboard Template Width: 12cm/4.7in

Clover Pompom Maker: Large (Light Blue, 3-3/8")

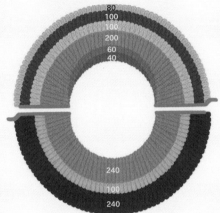

Trim the pompom into the shape of a hamburger. Trim lightly on top and heavy on the sides and bottom. On the side, leave the yarn that makes cheese and lettuce medium in length and cut the other yarns shorter to make this pompom look more realistic.

Letter – A

(See p.47 leftmost)

Type of Yarns: Fine – Green, Black

Cardboard Template Width: 6cm/2.4in

Clover Pompom Maker: Small (Yellow, 1-5/8")

Wrap yarn in the following order: 35 rounds of black, 10 rounds of green and then 20 rounds of black, etc. After finishing the lower layer, wrap a little green yarn on top of the black yarn on left-hand side and continue to wrap it until it touches the green yarn layer on the right. Trim the pompom and adjust the shape.

Letter – B

(See p.47 center)

Type of Yarns: Fine – White, Red

Cardboard Template Width: 6cm/2.4in

Clover Pompom Maker: Small (Yellow, 1-5/8")

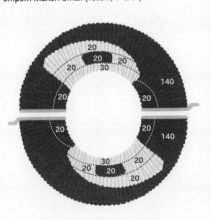

First, wrap 20 rounds of red yarn. Next wrap 30 rounds of white yarn according to the pattern. Wrapping the top white yarn thicker on the left side makes it easier to show the curves of the letter B. When using a pompom maker, pay particular attention to the directions. If you use a cardboard template for this pompom the letter on one side will always be upside-down.

Letter – C

(See p.47 rightmost)

Type of Yarns: Fine – White, Light Blue

Cardboard Template Width: 6cm/2.4in

Clover Pompom Maker: Small (Yellow, 1-5/8")

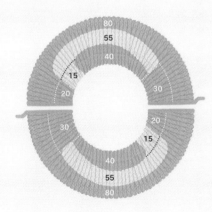

First, wrap 20 rounds of light blue, wrap less on the right side to make the letter round. Adjust the yarn to make the letter clear. With a pompom maker pay particular attention to the directions. If you use a template the letter on one side will always be upside-down.

89

Light - Light Brown   Light - Ocher

Apple – Core

(See p.34 left)
Type of Yarns: Fine – Red, Brown, Cream
Cardboard Template Width: 4cm/1.6in
Clover Pompom Maker: Small (Pink, 1-3/8")

Make the same two pompoms. Place the red part of one pompom on the top and the other on the bottom, then join them using brown yarn (see p. 59 for instructions on joining). Being careful not to cut the center yarn, trim the cream yarn down to form a scoop.

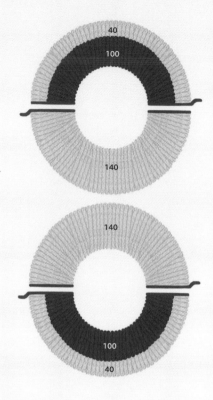

Apple – With a Bite

(See p.34 right)
Type of Yarns: Fine – Red, Brown, Cream
Cardboard Template Width: 9cm/3.5in
Clover Pompom Maker: Large (Green, 2-1/2")

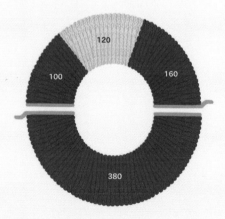

After you finish wrapping the pompom, tie the center with brown yarn. Trim the pompom into the shape of an apple. Cut the cream yarn down so it looks like someone has taken a bite.

Apple – Half

(See p.35)
Type of Yarns: Fine – Red, Brown, Cream
Cardboard Template Width: 9cm/3.5in
Clover Pompom Maker: Large (Green, 2-1/2")

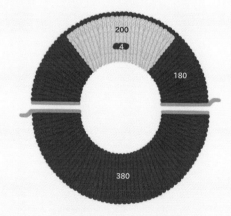

After you finish wrapping the pompom, tie the center with brown yarn. Trim half of the red part into the shape of apple and the other half, the cream part, to look like half of an apple.

Dharma Doll

(See p.48)
Type of Yarns: Fine – Off White, Red, Yellow, Black
Cardboard Template Width: 6cm/2.4in
Clover Pompom Maker: Small (Yellow, 1-5/8")
Cardboard Template Width: 9cm/3.5in
Clover Pompom Maker: Large (Green, 2-1/2")

For the head, wrap yarn according to the pattern. Leave the yarn used to tie the center a little bit long. After you finish wrapping the body, join the head to the body (see p.59 for instructions on joining). Trim the pompom using scissors. Adjust the shape of the pompom as you trim. Since the eyes easily shift position, adjust them using the tip of your scissors after wrapping.

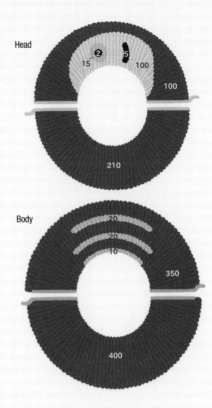

Bird

(See p.49 right)
Bird (See p.49 right)
Type of Yarns: Light – Blue Green
Cardboard Template Width: 4cm/1.6in
Clover Pompom Maker: Small (Pink, 1-3/8")

Make the same two pompoms and join them (see p.59 for instructions on joining). Trim the head smaller than the body. Glue colored craft wire on to the large pompom for legs. Glue a pair of wiggle eyes and a piece of colored craft plastic sheeting, for the beak, on the small pompom.

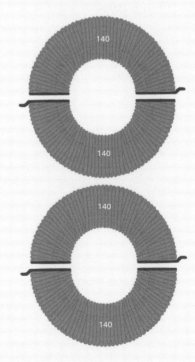

Glue on a pair of wiggle eyes.

Cut a sheet of colored craft plastic sheeting in the shape of beak. Bend it in half and glue it on.

Bend colored craft wire and make legs. Glue them on.

Light - Blue Green

Bird

(See p.49 center)
Type of Yarns: Fine – Brown
Cardboard Template Width: 4cm/1.6in
Clover Pompom Maker: Small (Pink, 1-3/8")

Make the same two pompoms and join them (see p.59 for instructions on joining). Trim the head smaller than the body. Without attaching the legs, trim the bottom short to make it look as if it were sitting. Glue on a piece of felt for a tail, a pair of wiggle eyes, and a piece of colored craft plastic sheeting for the beak.

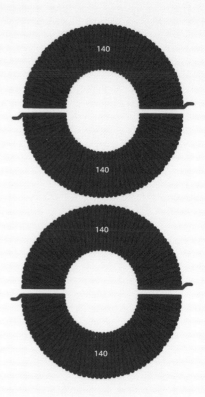

140

140

Glue on a pair of wiggle eyes.

Cut a piece of felt in a triangle shape and glue it on.

140

140

Cut a sheet of colored craft plastic sheeting in the shape of a beak and glue it on.

140

140

Bird

(See p.49 left)
Type of Yarns: Fine – Navy Blue
Cardboard Template Width: 4cm/1.6in
Clover Pompom Maker: Small (Pink, 1-3/8")

Make the same two pompoms and join them (see p.59 for instructions on joining). Trim the head smaller than the body. Glue on colored craft wire for legs, a pair of wiggle eyes, and a piece of colored craft plastic sheeting for the beak.

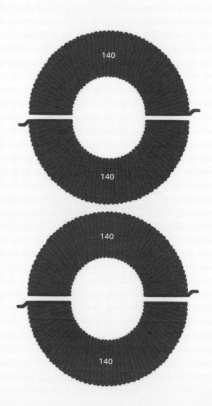

140

140

Glue on a pair of wiggle eyes.

Cut a piece of colored craft plastic sheeting in the shape of beak and glue it on.

Bend colored craft wire and make legs. Glue them on.

140

140

Hedgehog – Large

(See p.50 top)

Hedgehog – Large (See p.50 top)

Type of Yarns: Fine – Gray, Black / Light – Mixed Color

[Head]
Cardboard Template Width: 4cm/1.6in
Clover Pompom Maker: Small (Pink, 1-3/8")

[Body]
Cardboard Template Width: 6cm
Clover Pompom Maker: Small (Yellow, 1-5/8")

Join the head and the body (see p.59 for joining instructions.) Trim the pompom to make the nose pointy. Trim the yarn for hedgehog's hair so it appears rough. Using thick black yarn, sew on some eyes.

Head

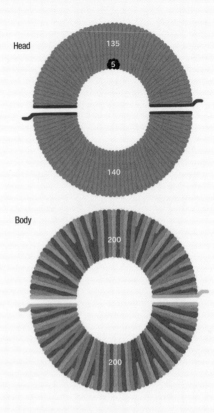

Body

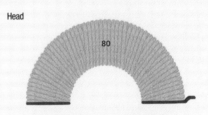

Hedgehog – Small

(See p.50 bottom left)

Type of Yarns: Fine – Beige / Light – Mixed Color
Cardboard Template Width: 4cm/1.6in
Clover Pompom Maker: Small (Pink, 1-3/8")

For the head, wrap yarn using one arm. Join the head and the body (see p.59 for joining instructions.) Trim the head quite a bit smaller than the body. Trim the pompom to make the nose pointy. Trim the yarn for hedgehog's hair so it appears rough. Using thick black yarn, sew on some eyes and using brown yarn, sew on a nose.

Head

Body

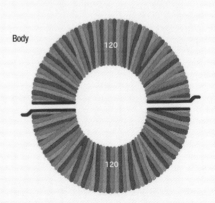

Light - Mixed Color

Ladybug

(See p.50 right)
Type of Yarns: Fine – Dark Red, Navy Blue
Cardboard Template Width: 4cm/1.6in
Clover Pompom Maker: Small (Pink, 1-3/8")

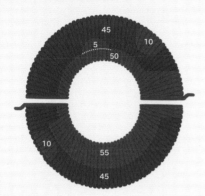

Make the top fluffy and trim the bottom flat. Tie the center of the pompom with navy blue thread, cut them to the desired length, and tie knots in the ends to make antennae.

Summer Scarf

(See p.51)
Type of Yarns: Super Fine
Cardboard Template Width: 9cm/3.5in
Clover Pompom Maker: Large (Green, 2-1/2")

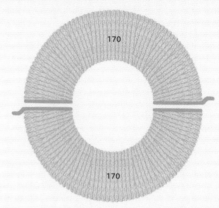

After removing the template, rinse the pompom with water to soften the yarn. While still wet, make the desired shape and hang to dry. When dried, the texture comes back. After drying put small dollops of glue at the center of the pompom and push each side of the pompom tightly to the side to hide the string used to tie the center of the pompom. This is non-washable yarn so attach the pompom so that it can be removed when you must wash the scarf.

Different Materials Pompom – Large

(See p.52, left)
Type of Yarns: Light (Leafy) – #751 / Fine – Mint /
              Manila Hemp Yarn – Coffee
Cardboard Template Width: 6cm/2.4in
Clover Pompom Maker: Large (Green, 2-1/2")

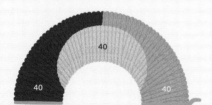

After wrapping your pompom, tie the center. Since the hemp comes off easily as is, be sure to secure the center of the pompom with glue before removing the pompom maker or cardboard template. You can make the hemp even more secure by applying more glue afterwards.

Different Materials Pompom – Small

(See p.52, right)
Type of Yarns: Light (Leafy) – #751 / Manila Hemp Yarn – Mint
Cardboard Template Width: 6cm
Clover Pompom Maker: Large (Green, 2-1/2")

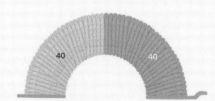

After wrapping your pompom, tie the center. Since the hemp comes off easily, be sure to secure the center of the pompom with glue before removing the pompom maker or template. You can make the hemp more secure by applying more glue afterwards. Compare with Different Material Pompom – Large. The number of rounds is decreased and there is only light trimming.

Super Fine   Light   Fine - Mint/Coffee

Different Materials Pompom

(See p.52, bottom)
Type of Yarns: Lilian (Super Fine)
Cardboard Template Width: 6cm/2.4in
Clover Pompom Maker: Small (Yellow, 1-5/8")

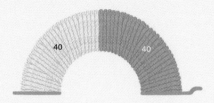

Since this yarn is slick and slippery, it is hard to wrap. Bundling four strings together and wrapping it in a lump makes it easier to wrap.

Pompom-sets

(See p.53)
Type of Yarns: Super Fine – Pink, Light Blue /
Hamanaka Rich Mohair Silk Fine – Light Purple /
Lace – Silver

* Prepare artificial flowers, leaves, and feathers that you like as well as a headdress base (a meshed bonnet base).

Cardboard Template Width: 4cm/1.6in
Clover Pompom Maker: Small (Pink, 1-3/8")
Cardboard Template Width: 6cm/2.4in
Clover Pompom Maker: Small (Yellow, 1-5/8")

For pink yarn, wrap 120 rounds,
for yellow yarn, wrap 200 rounds.

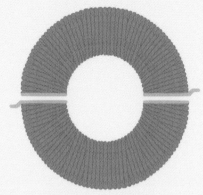

For pink yarn, wrap 120 rounds,
for yellow yarn, wrap 200 rounds.

Wrap yarn as desired and make several pompoms. Sew the pompoms onto a headdress base using sewing thread. Sew artificial flowers, leaves, and feathers onto the base while adjusting the balance as a whole. Attach a brooch pin at the back of the headdress base to complete. You can also attach a comb to make a different type of headdress.

Super Fine   Super Fine - Pink/Light Blue   Super Fine - Light Purple   Lace - Silver

Authors' Profiles

Pompoms

Four creators and designers who share a great deal of love for manual work and arts & crafts got together and formed this group. All members love books dearly and work in publication. They discuss, create, and enjoy making use of everyday objects for their crafts.

Kazue Kasuga

Born in 1968, she is president of "Bahar," a company that produces arts & crafts kits and books that introduce manual work and life in Eastern Europe. She was introduced to *matyo csavaritos kendo* — large pom pom hair accessories — while in Hungary and started to make pom poms soon thereafter.

Ryoko Nishizuka

Works for an advertising firm. She graduated from Musashino Art University in Visual Communication Design. She is a font designer who loves arts and crafts. She makes use of everyday objects to create various crafts. She also likes to collect materials such as fabrics, leather and buttons.

Naoko Nakui

She was born 1976 in Iwate prefecture. After graduating from Musashino Art University in Visual Communication Design, she worked for an advertising firm. In 2005, she became a freelancer. She produces paper related projects, mainly designing books. She toured the factory and was active as a reporter on the book entitled *Book Making Artisans*, published by Graphic-sha Co., Ltd.

Idea Oshima

He was born 1968 in Tochigi prefecture. He graduated from Tokyo Zōkei University in Design. Oshima produces fashion catalogues and designs books with a focus on movie and exhibition graphics.

Make Your Own Cute and Easy Pompoms
By Pompoms

First designed and published in Japan in 2011 by Graphic-sha Publishing Co., Ltd.
1-14-17 Kudankita, Chiyoda-ku, Tokyo 102-0073, Japan

Creative Publishing
international

First published in the United States of America by
Creative Publishing international, Inc., a member of
Quayside Publishing Group
400 First Avenue North
Suite 400
Minneapolis, MN 55401
1-800-328-3895
www.creativepub.com
Visit www.Craftside.Typepad.com for a behind-the-scenes peek at our crafty world!

ISBN: 978-1-58923-774-2

10 9 8 7 6 5 4 3 2 1

Book design:	Idea Oshima, Hayato Nakayama, Yumiko Ozeki
Photographs:	Makoto Haneda (PP. 01 to 53), Hirota Shashin Jimusho (PP.54-64)
Model:	Aiko Fukawa, Tamami Nishizuka, Pompom Nakui (dog)
Planning & Editing:	Junko Tsuda (Graphic-sha Publishing Co., Ltd.)

English edition
Layout:	Shinichi Ishioka
Translation:	Kevin Wilson
Production:	Kumiko Sakamoto (Graphic-sha Publishing Co., Ltd.)

Printed in China